YOUR KNOWLEDGE HAS VALUE

- We will publish your bachelor's and
  master's thesis, essays and papers

- Your own eBook and book -
  sold worldwide in all relevant shops

- Earn money with each sale

Upload your text at www.GRIN.com
and publish for free

Patrizia Koenig

Exploring Gombrich's "Art and Illusion" in Relation to the Philosophy of Science

GRIN Publishing

Bibliographic information published by the German National Library:

The German National Library lists this publication in the National Bibliography;
detailed bibliographic data are available on the Internet at http://dnb.dnb.de .

Imprint:

Copyright © 2012 GRIN Verlag GmbH
Print and binding: Books on Demand GmbH, Norderstedt Germany
ISBN: 978-3-656-43901-1

Progress in Arts & Science –
Exploring *E.H. Gombrich's 'Art and Illusion: A Study in the Psychology of Pictorial*
***Representation'* (1960) in Relation to the Philosophy of Science**

Patrizia Thuy Vi Koenig

University College Maastricht

December 9, 2012

1. Introduction

"Painting is a science and should be pursued as an inquiry into the laws of nature. Why, then, may not landscape painting be considered as a branch of natural philosophy, of which picture are but the experiments?" — John Constable (as cited in Gombrich, 1960, p. 29)

19th century British painter John Constable advocated the idea that through experimentation, art could rid itself of its chains of style and advance towards visual truth. With this notion he stands in a long Western tradition of viewing art progressing towards mimesis. To the same time the prevailing notion in science was that progress was the steady accumulation of established truths that would eventually provide access to a timeless world of reality. Progress was regarded as possessing a definite and unquestionable meaning, which was unique to the field of science[1]. This notion of 'progress' as a normative and goal-normative concept has come under scrutiny both in the arts and sciences (Niiniluoto, 2011).

In the history of art, Ernst Gombrich's groundbreaking *Art and Illusion: A Study in the Psychology of Pictorial Representation* (1960) was influential in arguing against the traditional view of representation of reality in art as imitation. In the philosophy of science, notably Karl Popper and then Thomas Kuhn challenged the concept of progress as the cumulation of factual observations. This paper wants to approach the larger issue of progress within the framework of *Art and Illusion* by asking: in how far do concepts of progress as derived from the philosophy of science relate to the notion of arts? More specifically, how did Gombrich challenge the traditional idea of representation as imitation? In following, it will be shown that Gombrich's methodology and main concepts are greatly indebted to Popper's theory of falsification. In a second step, Thomas Kuhn's theory of scientific revolution, which opposes Popper's writings, will be outlined in relation to Gombrich and his ideas of perception and classification.

2. Progress in Art & Science

2.1 "Making Precedes Matching" – Progress through Falsification

With *Art and Illusion*, Gombrich puts forward a comprehensive revision of the story of visual discoveries to answer the question why stylistic difference exists in different periods of time. He argues against the idea of mimesis as imitation, which goes back to Antiquity and continues well into the 19th century (Gombrich, 1960). Rejecting Ruskin's notion of the 'innocence of the eye' and the idea that stylistic change in art is the result of changes in straightforward modes of seeing and sense impressions, Gombrich draws on the psychology of representation to show how stylistic change is

---

[1] Philosopher of science George Staton defined science as: *"the history of science is the only history which can illustrate the progress of mankind. In fact, progress has no definite and unquestionable meaning in other fields than the field of science."* (Niiniluoto, 2011 p. 159)

rather dependent on the conceptual framework, the models and traditions in which the artist lives (ibid.).

The 'mental set' provides the artists with schemata, which determines what aspects of reality are perceived. The artist thus does not begin with some sense impressions, but with a hypothesis[2] – a horizon of expectation. As Gombrich explains ,

> *"Without some starting point, some initial schema, we could never get hold of the flux of experience. Without categories, we could not sort our impressions." (1960, p. 76)*

Yet an existing 'mental set' cannot be simply rejected and replaced by a new visual language. Only by subjecting it to a continuous process of 'making and matching' between the mental schemata and the natural world can man extend his awareness of the visible world (Jones, 2000; Gombrich, 1960).

Gombrich draws strong parallels with the philosophy of science: arguing against the synchronic notion of progress as the accumulation of sense impressions, he essentially advocates Popper's criticism towards induction - the 'bucket theory of the mind'. This largely 19th century synchronic belief suggests that it is possible to accumulate facts directly from sensory data, which will eventually develop the true picture of nature by means of logic. Under the ahistorical view of synchronic scientific investigation, it is assumed that everything in science, but also in art, can be experienced and that objective and passive observation is a trustworthy source for knowledge (McGuire, 2002).

In contrast, philosophers of science such as Karl Popper, Thomas Kuhn or Paul Feyerabend put forward a diachronic perspective of scientific change, which advocates the historical and social contingency of scientific change and the theory-ladeness of observations (Niiniluoto, 2011). Similarly, Gombrich suggests that any observation is considered the consequence of a question, and thereby guided by the expectations of a tentative hypothesis. Under this view, concepts of 'truth' and 'knowledge' are relative to the context out of which they arise. Hence, there is no atemporal method that will enable the scientist to arrive at a knowable reality or truth – rather, theory is constantly recontextualized.

The notion of progress is central Popper's theory of falsificationism: discarding the idea that theories can be shown to be true or probably true, progress takes the place of what truth was for the inductivists (Chalmers, 1999). Science advances through trial and error: problems lead to tentative theories, these are criticized and eventually falsified, leading to new problems (ibid.). Theories should be speculative conjectures that are to be rigorously tested by observation and experimental tests (ibid.). While Popper advocates that the secrets of the world can only be uncovered through novel and bold theories, he at the same time points out that there is no one criterion for truth to assess theories as legitimately true (Chalmers, 1999; Popper, 2002). Criteria of falsification – such as obscurity or incoherence – *may* allow the scientist to recognize error and falsity in a theory in a given historical context (Popper, 2002). Hence, falsificationists aim at the constant advancement of science through criticism, and less at the demonstration of truth (Chalmers, 1999). Withstanding severe testing and criticism can only indicate a high level of corrobation – never verification (Niiniluoto, 2011).

Gombrich similarly postulates that concepts, like pictures, can "only be more or less useful for the formation of descriptions", but never true or false (1960, p. 77). Applying Popper's trial and error model to the arts, Gombrich refers to this process as 'making and matching' – meaning that the creation of schemata precedes making. The artist constructs a hypothesis and tests it by stepping back from the canvas – pictorial representation becomes a sort of corroboration of the senses of order (Gombrich, 1982). Gombrich hence proposes a model of problem-solving for the development of Western art in which artists attempt to solve practical, technical problems (Wood, 2009).

Quoting Wölflinn, he advocates that paintings owe more to tradition than to direct observation (Gombrich, 1960). This echoes Popper's claim that while there are no ultimate sources of knowledge, the most important one is nevertheless is tradition (Popper, 2002). The artist cannot start from a tabula rasa, but must begin from an existing baseline from which he systematically compares, criticizes and improves upon the visual language of his predecessors (Gombrich, 1960). Artistic innovation is hence not merely the rejection of tradition, but a continuous and gradual process of experimentation, in which art becomes a tool for 'probing reality' against a set of invariants.

2.2 Kuhnian Paradigms & Progress

Thomas Kuhn's *The Structure of Scientific Revolutions* was published in 1962, two years after Gombrich's *Art and Illusion*[3]. While Gombrich desanctified the ideals of 'great art' by outlining its problem-solving activity, Kuhn similarly demonstrated that scientific knowledge was collective and conventional by nature, "driven by ambition and limited by force of habit" (Wood, 2009, p. 837). With *The Structure of Scientific Revolutions,* however, Kuhn challenges the inductivist *and* falsificationist view of science on the basis that both do not hold up regarding historical evidence (Chalmers, 1999). Kuhn, as Popper, opposes the synchronic view that scientific progress is not a continuous process of accumulating empirical evidence and content and that there is no objective criterion for truth (Niiniluoto, 2011). However, Kuhn puts forward a definition of progress that differs greatly from Popper's idea that consecutive theories may advance towards the truth (ibid). Generally, Kuhn explains the notion of progress in terms of scientific revolutions as contingent of its socio-historical and temporal context (Chalmers, 1999).

Hereby the 'paradigm' plays a central role: it is a conceptual framework shared by a scientific community, which consists of a general standard of theoretical laws and assumptions that are applied with an accepted form of methodology and instruments (ibid.). Under the rules of this single

---

[3] Commenting at a later point in time on the relation between his writing on progress in science, and the arts, Kuhn refers to Gombrich's work as a great source of encouragement (1969). As he points out, topics such as the nature of innovation or changing modes of perception have a long tradition in the history of art, but are only minimally represented in the history of science.

paradigm, scientists practice 'normal science', which allows them to engage in puzzle-solving activity of theoretical and experimental nature[4].

Although Kuhn's ambivalence towards scientific progress makes a coherent picture of 'Kuhnian progress' difficult, one can delineate two different kinds of progress in his theory. On the one hand, it may be considered as the capacity of theories to solve ever more puzzles that are generated by the paradigm within a period of normal science. As criticism and severe testing of theory experience a period of relaxation during normal science, working within such a paradigm allows the scientist to engage in detailed work that is necessary to improve the match between paradigm and nature (Kuhn, 1962).

On the other hand, science progresses through paradigm shifts – the replacement of paradigms through scientific revolutions. The latter notion of progress takes place once the existing paradigm loses more and more of its puzzle-solving ability, whereby anomalies begin to pose serious problems to the very fundament of the paradigm. The resulting crisis opens the field for critical debate. An incommensurable rival paradigm will develop out of this, which will view different questions and general standards as legitimate, and also perceive the world differently (ibid.). Once the existing paradigm is abandoned for another one by a scientific community based on conviction, one can speak of a scientific revolution. In this sense, progress is not viewed as continual, but as rare episodes of revolution in science. Whereas for Popper progress is a continual refutation of theories towards the truth – also termed 'evolutionary epistemology' – Kuhn suggests a non-cumulative advance of science through 'selection by conflict' (Chalmers, 1999; Jones, 2000)[5].

Despite Gombrich's sympathies for Popper's methodology, his concept of the 'mental set' can also be considered in terms of the Kuhnian paradigm. Just as the paradigm structures the scientist's perception of observation and prescribes the scientist's field of research, the mental set articulates a system of schemata that are to the artist's disposal. For both Kuhn and Gombrich, models of perception or schemata are dependant on experience, practice/training, and attitudes (Wood, 2009; Kuhn, 1962). The paradigm provides scientists with a criterion for choosing these problems, and guides the scientist in the search for and interpretation of observations and experiments (Kuhn, 1962).

The radical switch within a new paradigm – termed the 'Gestalt switch'– brings with it a revolutionary change in ways of seeing. Yet while Gombrich views the development of new mental sets as the continuous process of 'making and matching', Kuhn considers the advancement of paradigms as a radical overthrow – rendering it incommensurable to other paradigm. Kuhn shows how paradigms control scientific perception and as different paradigms can be regarded as different worldviews, they also cannot be compared in terms of perception (1962). This clearly makes it difficult to assess different paradigms from the perspective of progressiveness. Similarly the issue that the past is never definitively denied in the arts makes clear the limits of Kuhn's model for

---

[4] Kuhn's use of the term 'puzzle' refer to a special category of problems that test the skill in solution, but that are not necessarily intrinsically interesting (Kuhn, 185).

understanding artistic change. As philosopher Maarten Doorman points out, *"theories displace one another, works of art enrich one another"*(2003, p. 133).

3. Conclusion

How, then, can one view Gombrich's concept of progress within the framework of the philosophy of science? It has been shown that for Gombrich shares Popper's and Kuhn's criticism towards the synchronic view of progress as the accumulation of sense impressions towards an mind-independent truth. Although Gombrich acknowledges the existence of stylistic advances in representational art, he explicitly rejects Hegelian notion of progress in art as 'Zeitgeist", of the refinement of the spirit of the age (Wood, 2009). He rather suggests that revolutions in art are driven by individuals, and that one's awareness of the world is extended through process of 'making and matching'. This concept is clearly indebted to Popper's theory of falsification.

At the same time, however, it has been shown that the mental set closely relates to the contingency of perception in the Kuhnian paradigm. Stylistic changes in art are hence not due to improvements in imitation, but due to changed systems of classification. In a sense, Kuhn's concept of progress as the increasing ability to solve puzzles within a paradigm is applicable to Gombrich's view of the development of the mental set. However, Kuhn's other concept of non-cumulative progress in science as the replacement of an old paradigm by another incommensurable one, speaks against Gombrich's view of progress. Indeed, Gombrich postulates that artistic change is much more than the rejection of tradition, but is a process of experimentation that begins from an existing baseline.

Yet what happens when art abandons the value of mimesis and painterly skills, and thereby any falsifiable criteria? It is here that Gombrich's view of progress in the visual representation of art as continual refutation seems to reach its limits. In its place, Kuhn's theory of scientific revolutions has found widespread application for understanding postmodern art. However, the incommensurability of Kuhnian paradigms makes the applicability of his theory onto the arts difficult. What should one then make out of the concept of progress in the arts? Is it even possible to talk of progress anymore, have we arrived at the 'end of art' as Arthur Danto famously proclaimed? Maarten Doorman rejects this neo-Hegelian perspective in arguing that,

> *"The very possibility of progress creates a pattern in the cacophony of the present. The question of whether a work of art adds something to history is still not a useless one – as long as it remains free of modernistic pedantry and avant-gardist dogmatism" (2003, p.144)*

If one holds on to the idea of progress as a legitimate and important concept in the contemporary arts, then a new understanding of progress is pivotal. Despite the limitations of Gombrich's account of visual representation for postmodern art, his notion of progress as a process of accumulation is a useful framework for understanding how contemporary art does not exist in a incommensurable paradigm but, in fact, stands in a complex relationship to the art of the past.

Bibliography

Chalmers, A.F. (1999). *What is this thing called Science?* Cambridge, MA: Hacket Publishing Company.

Doorman, M. (2003): *Art in Progress. A Philosophical Response to the End of the Avant-Garde.* Amsterdam: Amsterdam University Press.

Gombrich, E.H. (1960). *Art & Illusion: A Study in the Psychology of Pictorial Representation.* London: Phaidon.

Gombrich, E.H. (1982). *What I Learned from Karl Popper, In Pursuit of Truth.* Atlantic Highlands NJ: Humanities Press, 203–20.

Jones, C.A. (2000). The Modernist Paradigm. *Critical Inquiry*, 2 (26), 488–528.

Kuhn, T. (1962). The Structure of Scientific Revolutions. Chicago: University of Chicago Press.

McGuire, J.E. (2002) Scientific Change: Perspectives and Proposals. In Merrilee H. Salmon (Ed.), *Introduction to the Philosophy of Science: A Text by Members of the Department of History and Philosophy of Science of the University of Pittsburgh.* Englewood Cliffs, N.J.: Prentice Hall.

Niiniluoto, I. (Summer 2011). "Scientific Progress", *The Stanford Encyclopedia of Philosophy.* Edward N. Zalta (ed.), retrieved December 9, 2012, <http://plato.stanford.edu/archives/sum2011/entries/scientific-progress/>.

Popper, K. (2002) On the Sources of Knowledge and Ignorance, in *Conjectures and Refutations: The Growth of Scientific Knowledge.* 3-35. London: Routledge

Wood, C.S. (2009, December). E.H. Gombirch's 'Art and Illusion: A Study in the Psychology of Pictorial Representation', 1960. *The Burlington Magazine.*